MR P'S WEEKLY IDEA

GIVING PRIMARY SCHOOL TEACHERS SOMETHING TO CONSIDER FOR THE WEEK AHEAD...

BY JAMIE PARKINSON

Sometimes the mind just needs a few words to focus on a potential solution ...

I hope this book helps to give you that focus.

LIGHTBULBS ARE HERE!

Welcome to the world of simple ideas for a big impact! This book contains a multitude of ideas based on different scenarios that might help to focus your mind for the week ahead.

Whether you are looking for simple advice to help children in your class, or you are keen to attack some of your own practice, this book is divided into sections housing ideas to suit various points in the academic year.

WHEN SHOULD I READ THIS?

Sunday evening can often be a time where the mind of a teacher can become engulfed with stresses and strains of the coming week. With three ideas per section, this book can give you a counter thought for those moments, starting your week with a desire to implement a simple idea for a big classroom impact...

Let creativity reign free!

Good luck!

CONTENTS

CONTENTS

1
STARTING A NEW YEAR

Starting a new year can be a daunting time for both the children and the teacher.

Whatever happens at the start of the year will lay a foundation that is hard to alter, so it is important we get it right...

STARTING A NEW YEAR

Don't be afraid to share your holiday experiences with the children!

It is great for them to hear that you are not just a robot who lives in the school, and that you actually have a life and family of your own outside of the school walls!

STARTING A NEW YEAR

Continue to reflect on your experiences from last year. What did you do well? What are you proud of? What would you like to improve?

Set yourself some achievable goals outside of your Performance Management that can be achieved in a given timeframe.

STARTING A NEW YEAR

Get to know your timetable really well, decide how you will be able to effectively manage all of your weekly tasks and add these to the timetable.

Be conscious of assessment and ensure that you have considered how much time will be needed on each day.

2
THE EXTRA MILE

The difference between good teachers and great teachers is the extra mile. Great teachers achieve great results by considering that little bit extra...

THE EXTRA MILE

This week spend some time on the gate in the morning.

Seeing how and when the children arrive at school can often explain their mood when they arrive in the classroom.

THE EXTRA MILE

Focus your attention on lunchtimes this week...maybe sit and have lunch with the children.

The conversations are so much more different to classroom natter, and you can also learn more about friendship groups that may not already know!

THE EXTRA MILE

Remember to spend some time discussing what the children have been up to over the weekend!

They will want to share their stories with you and their classmates ... be sure to allow time for everybody though!

3
START OF THE DAY

The start of the day will clearly define the path that the rest of the day will take. Getting this bit right will significantly impact the outcomes as the day goes on...

START OF THE DAY

Arrive at school a little earlier than usual this week and see what else you can achieve.

You will be amazed at the amount you can get done in a short space of time when there are less distractions!

START OF THE DAY

Each day is a new day. You may not have had success with your time last week so set yourself the target of achieving more this week.

Don't dwell on what could have been achieved, focus on what <u>will</u> be achieved!

START OF THE DAY

Spend some time chatting to the children as they are lining up during the course of this week.

Simply making your way along the class line and greeting them individually will help to kickstart the day in a positive way!

4
THE BEHAVIOUR MYSTERIES

It can often appear a mystery why a child behaves the way they do.

Consider some slight adjustments to your week to try and unravel that mystery...

THE BEHAVIOUR MYSTERIES

Pop out and do an extra duty to monitor who the children are playing with, if anyone.

It could give you an invaluable understanding as to what could be triggering that behaviour...

THE BEHAVIOUR MYSTERIES

Get to know the children individually, maybe do a 'quiz' to learn more about their hobbies and interests.

Using this knowledge to direct tasks in class could really help them to come out of their shell a little!

THE BEHAVIOUR MYSTERIES

Complete a paired work activity this week but give the children a 'role' – one as speaker, one as listener.

The children need to share some of their interests in one minute. You can then learn more about the children in your class as you listen in to their conversations.

5
HELP OUT A COLLEAGUE

The greatest gift you can give, and for anyone to receive, is a random act of kindness. Consider your colleagues this week and if you sense someone needs a 'lift' give one of these ideas a go...

HELP OUT A COLLEAGUE

Think of something that you would like someone else to do for you.

Why not cover a break duty, or complete some photocopying for them? Maybe mark some books or make them a cup of tea? Being given these gifts can really help to give a little lift...

HELP OUT A COLLEAGUE

Is one of your colleagues leading a staff meeting for the first time?

They might look confident, but a little support will go a long way. Offer to listen to what they have prepared and help with any last-minute organisational issues that they may have.

HELP OUT A COLLEAGUE

Have you prepared some whiteboard slides that you think others could use as a starting block?

Share your creative flair and give your colleagues a helping hand along the way.

6
OUTSIDE OF THE BOX!

Creativity cannot be underestimated in the world of teaching! Considering an idea that takes you out of your comfort zone can often be where the magic of learning can really happen...

OUTSIDE OF THE BOX!

This week, why not allow various children time to deliver the starter/plenary of lessons? Yes, I mean let them teach parts of the lesson!

The impact? A great assessment tool and a brilliant way to build a child's self esteem ...

OUTSIDE OF THE BOX!

Have a go at mixing up the register a little bit!

Maybe ask the children to answer with what they had for dinner last night, rather than "good morning!"

This is a little bit of fun but you can also get a useful insight into home life too!

OUTSIDE OF THE BOX!

It is time to mix up your assessment!

Ask the children to share the work of a peer and explain why it's great!

Feeling creative? Airdrop their work to your Interactive Whiteboard and show all of the children close up what has been a success!

7
NEGATIVE TO POSITIVE

It is far too often that negative scenarios can take over. It takes time and patience, but if you can transform a negative to positive, you have immediately flipped the resulting outcome...

NEGATIVE TO POSITIVE

Focus on those children where you normally have to phone parents for a negative reason.

See how their week goes and aim to call each parent with positive news by Friday. What a difference this will make to their weekend, as well as the following week!

NEGATIVE TO POSITIVE

This idea considers the gloomy nature that January can bring, both for teachers and for the children in the class!

Often these are testing times and the children begin to challenge relentlessly, but maintain that calm approach. The calmer you are, the calmer they will be, and the more successful your lessons will be.

NEGATIVE TO POSITIVE

Is there a child that has been in trouble at break times?

Focus on any positives you hear from other children and then celebrate this in front of the rest of the class – keeping this consistent with all of the children can make a big difference.

8
WEEKLY CHALLENGES

Keeping homework tasks fresh will keep the children interested! These challenges could be used as homework or as an extra task for the children to complete with their family at home!

WEEKLY CHALLENGES

This week encourage your children to read a little more at home.

Set them a challenge, maybe pages to read in a week, and ask them to report back at the end of the week - preferably with a note from home to report back on success too!

WEEKLY CHALLENGES

Are there any times tables that your class has generally struggled with? Complete a quiz on Monday to see what they score. Quiz again on the Friday of the same week and reward the children for any improvement, including a message home!

Don't forget to reward those ones who maintain 100% correct!

WEEKLY CHALLENGES

Challenge the children to find out about a member of their family - possibly a grandparent who they do not know a lot about?

Set aside some time at the end of the week for the children to feedback to the class!

9
CREATIVE IDEAS

It is good practice to consider how improvements can be made.

Varying your delivery every now and again, or choosing a slightly different activity/ resource helps to maintain the children's attention...

CREATIVE IDEAS

Before sending the children out to break, ask them a multiplication question. If they get it right they can go, if they get it wrong they will have to wait for another question!

This will encourage them to continue learning their tables and will help the class leave in an orderly fashion!

CREATIVE IDEAS

Are you looking at story writing this week? Why not try some free comic builder software online?

This is a great way to encourage the children to consider elements of a story and plan the events carefully.

CREATIVE IDEAS

Teaching fractions often brings out the pizza diagrams and paper segments...

Try bringing real pizza in and using that for a truly immersive learning experience!

10
REGULAR ROUTINES

Having routines that are specific to your class will help them to prepare for a week ahead. Keeping these 'regular routines' will really encourage the children to take ownership of their own learning...

REGULAR ROUTINES

Spend some time talking to your class about what books they are reading at home.

Do they have any favourite authors?

Give them some time to discuss books with friends and then research the authors online.

REGULAR ROUTINES

One person's junk is another person's treasure!

Regularly send a message out to the parents of your school and ask if they are going to be throwing any toys away...

These toys can become brilliant props for your animation lessons in ICT!

REGULAR ROUTINES

Consistency is the key to success! If you are rewarding the class, for scoring 100% on their weekly spellings for example, make sure you keep that reward consistent throughout the year. They will strive for it!

If you don't do it one week their commitment may well drop!

11
SATS

Test week in schools is always a difficult time but it is important to consider the impact on all parties. Concentrate on how you can make these weeks as bearable as possible!

SATS

Preparing for the test week is important but consider different ways of revising.

Allow the children opportunities on devices, not just using past papers, and explore areas of the curriculum that they themselves are less confident with.

SATS

Remembering the stress that the children are under for the SATs is important, but also remember how important 'normality' is...

Letting standards slip will inevitably affect behaviour, which will be no good for anyone!

SATS

Consider an activity project that the children would really enjoy following the test week.

Link objectives in to give the children a learning experience that is much less intense than the week they have had to endure.

12
INSPECTIONS

Inspections are never easy but they can be made more comfortable with a lot of careful consideration and strategic planning.

When that call arrives, stay calm and start those strategic thought processes...

INSPECTIONS

Don't try and do anything too complex or new that you would not normally do with the class.

Firstly, the children may call you on it, and secondly it will not be familiar to you.

Just be yourself and know that you are a great teacher!

INSPECTIONS

Consider this an opportunity to prove what a good teacher you are.

Use your nerves to your advantage and focus on demonstrating how well you know your class and how best you can teach them. Try to enjoy the experience of showing someone how good you are at your job!

INSPECTIONS

Remember all of the success you have had with your class and don't panic.

Be well prepared for every lesson and have a strategy in place to ensure your assessment is completed in reasonable time – draw out a timetable if necessary.

Good luck!

13
CLASS ASSEMBLY

Planning and delivering a class assembly can be one of most enjoyable but stressful times of the year!

Just remember what it is for and plan each element with careful consideration ...

CLASS ASSEMBLY

Before selecting your theme, have a really detailed discussion with your class to ascertain who wants which part.

Do not guarantee anything to start with but this knowledge of what they actually want to do will help when assigning roles!

CLASS ASSEMBLY

Consider including a variety of activities in your assembly - reading, acting, singing, dancing etc...

Not only will this keep the audience interested, it will also allow more children an opportunity to demonstrate their talents!

CLASS ASSEMBLY

For some children this will be their first time performing, or it may be that they have never put themselves forward for a role before.

There will need to be careful guidance and encouragement, so be sure to celebrate the confidence and bravery of the children during rehearsals.

14
TIME MANAGEMENT

One of the key skills of a successful teacher is the ability to manage time, and create windows of opportunity that others never knew existed...

TIME MANAGEMENT

PPA time is invaluable, but use it wisely! On those days consider what you would like to achieve in your PPA and stick to it.

Be aware, of course, that this time could be disrupted should you need to deal with anything new that may have arisen that you were not expecting!

TIME MANAGEMENT

Spend a week altering part of your usual routine to see if you can save time.

Avoid the staffroom during your PPA - it is inevitable you will be distracted and could end up in conversations that may eat away at your precious time!

TIME MANAGEMENT

Try marking some books during break times this week and see what difference this makes.

You will have put a dent in your marking load and it may also allow you some time to leave a little earlier!

15
USE OF ICT

Using ICT can transform your lessons and really enhance the delivery.

Whilst every lesson may not need a revamp, you could elevate those lessons that need just that little extra in them...

USE OF ICT

Preparing your whiteboard for the day ahead will not only keep you organised but it will also help the lessons flow more freely.

Prepare your usual dates and titles, but spend some time linking all of your resources to objects and images on the slides - you will be amazed at the difference when you do not have to keep travelling to the computer!

USE OF ICT

Do you have a child who is a reluctant writer? If so, why not explore the use of recording film as a form of assessment? Ask them to deliver answers to you in a video rather than in writing.

Using this as part of the celebration of work in front of the class will help to raise that child's confidence and encourage them more in the future.

USE OF ICT

Use a camera to take photos of work throughout the lesson. You can either share these to the whiteboard through the device, or plug the camera into the PC.

You can now demonstrate how to edit work 'live' in the lesson, giving the children a clear direction when they are editing their own work.

16
PARENTS EVENING

P arents evening is one of the most important nights of the year as it will dictate much of the correspondence that will follow between the teacher and the family...

PARENTS EVENING

As with all elements of a school year, preparation is paramount for a successful evening.

Prepare notes for what you would like to say, but avoid sentences as this will encourage you to read rather than interact throughout the meeting.

PARENTS EVENING

Always begin the meeting with "how do you think things are going then?"

This allows them to raise a point first. You want the parent to be listening to everything you are saying but if they have something on their mind from the outset they are unlikely to digest all of what you are saying until they have raised their issue.

PARENTS EVENING

Make your table neat, tidy and welcoming for when you are meeting the parents. Why not have a basket of chocolates for them to help themselves?

This creates a positive environment for everyone from the beginning!

17
CLASSROOM IDEAS

Making your classroom individual to you and your class gives the children a real sense of ownership. Considering the impact of even the smallest elements of your classroom can make a big difference...

CLASSROOM IDEAS

Why not try something new for the names of your tables? Consider naming each after characters from your favourite film, or your favourite foods?

It creates a fun environment whilst making it individual to you and the class!

CLASSROOM IDEAS

Do you have a cupboard door, or spare piece of wall space?

Paint it black and you will be able to use it as an 'ideas and questions' chalkboard, giving the children ownership to add to it when they wish!

CLASSROOM IDEAS

Set an alarm on your classroom computer so that you know when each of the children have a birthday throughout the year!

You can then write a message on the board for them to see when they arrive in school!

18
SELF-LED CPD

The world of education will never stand still, so teachers should continue reflecting on, as well as potentially leading, their own CPD to further enhance their practice...

SELF-LED CPD

Whilst PPA is like 'Golden Time' to a teacher, consider using a portion of time to observe a colleague.

Every teacher has a unique style and it is always interesting to observe others to gain any handy hints that might be useful!

SELF-LED CPD

Spend some time this week focussing on a book, maybe a recommendation from your line manager.

You could find some key answers to some questions that may have been circling your mind!

SELF-LED CPD

Research some education blogs online, and maybe even become an active participant!

If you discover anything useful, email it to yourself at work - that way you are more likely to do something with it than if it was just notes written on a piece of paper!

19
CREATIVE MARKING

We all know how much of our week is taken up with marking, but also how important it is. Don't be afraid to try some different strategies when attacking assessment...

CREATIVE MARKING

When planning your lessons this week, be sure to allocate some time within the lesson to mark with groups of children.

Marking with the children in the lesson not only gives them on-the-spot feedback but you also have less books in your pile at the end of the day!

CREATIVE MARKING

This is not an excuse to pass your marking over, but a legitimate opportunity to share work!

Ask the children to mark each other's work - this will encourage them to look for errors (which will help them to remember these errors themselves!) and will also enable them to read first hand some good examples of what you are expecting!

CREATIVE MARKING

The use of stickers in marking can be an extremely useful way to assess the understanding of the children and move them on.

Print the stickers prior to the lesson and add in an extra question for them to try at the start of the next lesson. This takes less time than 'marking' and will give the child a clear reflection of what is expected of them to move their learning on further.

20
REWARDS

It is always a great incentive to offer rewards to the children for their work.

As with any expectation, consistency will be the key to any success...

REWARDS

Start rewarding the children for brilliant work with a raffle ticket!

At the end of each half term hold a draw of the raffle tickets and award a special prize to some winners!

REWARDS

Focus on rewarding children for their homework this week.

Pick a brilliant piece each day and allow that child to sit at your desk for the day. The children will really enjoy this privilege!

REWARDS

If you ask the children what their favourite time of the day is, many of them would say "break time!"

Why not offer an extra break time to those children that achieve a given set of objectives?

21
END OF THE YEAR

The end of a school year presents many challenges for a teacher so it is important to remember those key time management principles to keep you afloat!

END OF THE YEAR

Now is the time of year where things can start to mount up - reports, end of year shows, assessments etc...

Make sure you manage your time well.

You need to remember that a healthy mind is a healthy teacher!

END OF THE YEAR

Spend some time having a review session with your class – what do they think they have done well and what do they think they could improve upon for next year?

Give the children an opportunity to share in the successes of their classmates too!

END OF THE YEAR

Why not create a memories movie, where each of the children give 2 things that they are really proud of, or that they have really enjoyed?

You could link them all together and then produce a short film with music too!

Sharing this with the class will be a great way to end the year.

22
SCHOOL HOLIDAYS

There will often be much excitement as the school holidays approach so why not offer the children opportunities to share memories with their classmates...

SCHOOL HOLIDAYS

In the lead up to the holidays, complete a lesson where the children give examples of their favourite things they have done in the past.

The children will enjoy sharing their memories but it will also give them some ideas for the next holiday too!

SCHOOL HOLIDAYS

Collate a list of websites/activities that give parents some ideas for things to do over the summer!

They will really appreciate having these options but this could also give the children some practical learning opportunities too!

SCHOOL HOLIDAYS

Consider setting your future class an optional challenge of completing a diary over the school holiday that can be shared with the class when they return.

This is a great way to get to know the children better from day one!

23
WORKING DURING HOLIDAYS

It is inevitable that you will need to work over the school holidays, but it is important to remember that the holiday is for you as much as it is for the children...

WORKING DURING HOLIDAYS

Plan your holiday time well and focus on specific tasks that are achievable.

Setting an unrealistic target will set you up to fail which will affect your confidence when the holiday has finished.

WORKING DURING HOLIDAYS

During the half term break, ignore those cries of "I'll just do one more lesson plan..." or "let's plan a brand new unit... why not..."

Plan what is absolutely needed for when you return and then take some time off, refresh the mind and have a well earned break!

WORKING DURING HOLIDAYS

As the last week of the summer arrives, take some time for yourself.

Don't kid yourself into thinking that working will help you after the break... recharging your batteries is the best work you can do from this point on - enjoy the rest of the holiday!

OVER TO YOU!

Now that you have read the ideas why not give them a try! Focussing the mind on one specific area will help you to combat and improve those elements that may have been challenging last week. Every week can present a new challenge, but these challenges are always surmountable when you put your mind to it.

If you are having one of those 'Sunday night moments' pick the book up again and head straight to the section that will help you most ... it may offer that little bit of guidance that can put you on the path to achieving success.

Good luck!

ABOUT THE AUTHOR

Jamie Parkinson is a freelance education and workplace consultant, author and copywriter. His previous role was E-Learning Leader and Pupil Premium Champion in a junior school in West Sussex. This saw Jamie leading the development of 21st century technology as a focus for improving pupil outcomes. He has 13 years of Leadership experience, working as a Year Leader prior to his E-Learning position.

A husband and father to two boys, he enjoys going on adventures with the family, including visits to theme parks! As well as writing, Jamie enjoys running and singing.

Jamie has co-written the popular "The Things They Didn't Teach You At Uni: a guide to being an NQT" with colleague and friend Luke Osborne.

Printed in Great Britain
by Amazon

11859975R00059